ALTERNATOR BOOKS™

PICTURES to PARAGRAPHS

WRITING A PERSONAL NARRATIVE

Brianna Kaiser

Lerner Publications ◆ Minneapolis

Lerner Publications Company
An imprint of Lerner Publishing Group, Inc.
241 First Avenue North
Minneapolis, MN 55401 USA

For reading levels and more information, look up this title at www.lernerbooks.com.

Main body text set in Aptifer Sans LT Pro.
Typeface provided by Linotype AG.

Editor: Angel Kidd **Designer:** Emily Harris **Photo Editor:** Angel Kidd
Lerner team: Martha Kranes

Library of Congress Cataloging-in-Publication Data

Names: Kaiser, Brianna, 1996– author
Title: Writing a personal narrative / Brianna Kaiser.
Description: Minneapolis : Alternator Books, 2026. | Series: Pictures to Paragraphs (Alternator Books) | Includes bibliographical references and index. | Audience: Ages 8–12 | Audience: Grades 4–6 | Summary: "Photos can call to mind powerful memories. By using images as catalysts for their own narratives, readers will learn how to write about their lives and the process that goes with writing a personal narrative"—Provided by publisher.
Identifiers: LCCN 2025013249 (print) | LCCN 2025013250 (ebook) | ISBN 9798765688762 library binding | ISBN 9798348028756 paperback | ISBN 9798765695784 epub
Subjects: LCSH: Autobiography—Authorship—Juvenile literature | Biography as a literary form—Juvenile literature | LCGFT: Autobiographies
Classification: LCC CT25 .K25 2026 (print) | LCC CT25 (ebook) | DDC 808.06/692—dc23/eng/20250401

LC record available at https://lccn.loc.gov/2025013249
LC ebook record available at https://lccn.loc.gov/2025013250

Manufactured in the United States of America
1-1012671-54706-5/20/2025

TABLE OF CONTENTS

TELLING YOUR STORY

A teacher calls out a student's name. The student holds a sheet of paper as they walk to the front of the classroom. They clear their throat and begin to read from the paper: "This is the story of the time I . . ."

There are many forms of writing and ways to tell stories. Personal narratives are stories of a writer's real or imagined experiences. Memoirs and autobiographies are some examples. Each narrative has a beginning, middle, and end.

The writing process of personal narratives includes three stages. In the first stage, writers plan and draft their story. They think about what they are going to write about, and then they write the first version of their story.

In the second stage, writers share their story with peers, such as other students in their class. After writers get peer feedback, they evaluate their story and revise it. In the third stage, writers finish editing their story, and then they may publish it. Let's learn more about what to do in these stages and use photo prompts to inspire your writing.

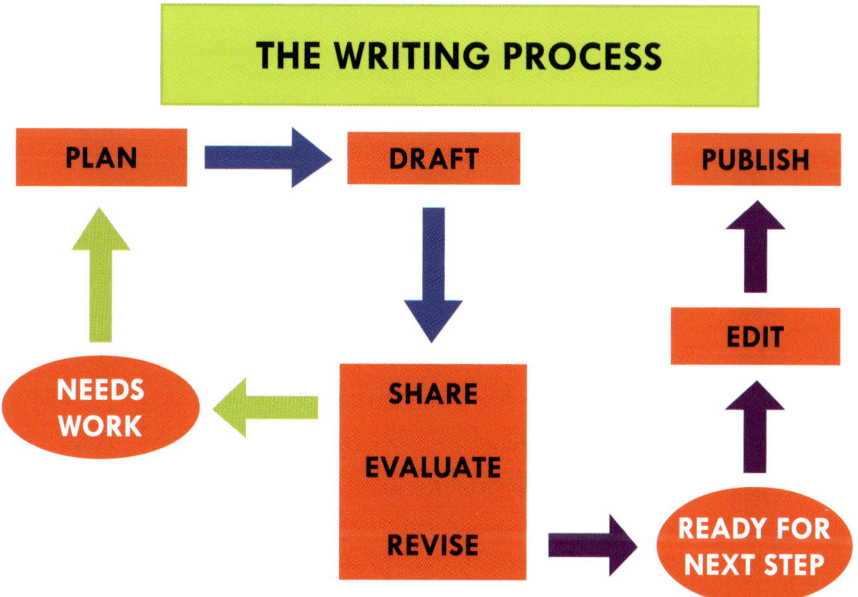

CHAPTER 1
THE BEGINNING

Before writing your story, you should plan it. Think about a story from your life that you want to tell. Remember, a personal narrative is something you have experienced or imagine yourself experiencing. This type of writing can be fictional, but it is usually based on true events.

Once you have a story idea, create an outline with a beginning, middle, and end. Add any events or people you think you may need to include to help tell your story. It is okay if your story changes after you begin writing. The outline is just to help you think about your story in more detail.

After you finish your outline, you can begin writing a first draft. The first draft is the first version of your story and does not need to be polished. It is a chance for you to experiment with writing your ideas and have fun. To get started on your draft, you will need to think about an order of events, a point of view, and how to write an engaging introduction.

A personal narrative can take place anywhere.

Your story should have a clear order of events. That is why your story outline needs to include a beginning, middle, and end. When you write a personal narrative, you are trying to help readers understand and follow what you experienced. If you tell the story in a disorganized order, the reader may get lost or confused.

WRITING PROMPT: ORDER OF EVENTS

Think about a vacation or day trip that you have taken with your family or friends. To outline the beginning of your story, write about where you went and how you got there. To outline the middle of the story, write about what you did during the trip. To outline the end of your story, write about how this trip ended.

Once you have an outline, think about your story's point of view. Personal narratives are usually told from the point of view of the narrator or main character, which is often the person writing the story. They are also usually told in first person. First person stories are told with the pronouns *I*, *me*, *my*, *we*, and *our*. You should also choose if you will write your story in past tense or present tense. Past tense is something that has already happened. Present tense is something that is currently happening.

WRITING PROMPT: POINT OF VIEW

Imagine you are one of the people at this birthday party and write a narrative from their point of view. Are you writing the story as a guest at the party, or are you writing the story as the birthday person? How does changing the point of view change the kind of story you may write?

The first part of your personal narrative is the beginning, or introduction. The beginning should engage the reader and make them want to keep reading your story. It should set up the scene by including a location, a main character (usually yourself), and some kind of action the main character will take or journey they will go on. Your story may also include other characters. These could be people from your life, such as friends and family.

WRITING PROMPT: ENGAGING INTRO

Consider this moment at a soccer game. What is happening? Why is this moment going to be important to the rest of the story? Now think about a big moment from your life, such as making a play in a sporting event or performing in a recital. Write about why that moment was important in that specific story from your life.

CHAPTER 2

WHAT COMES NEXT

After planning and writing the beginning of your story, it is time to write the middle of it, which is made up of body paragraphs. Body paragraphs carry your story forward and share more information about your journey. Your story can end with the conclusion of this journey, or it can look forward to how it may conclude in the future. With a beginning, middle, and end, you have a first draft.

Sharing your first draft with peers is the next part of the writing process. After you get their feedback, evaluate or review your story for anything that you may need to change to make it stronger. Look at details, dialogue, and more to help strengthen your story. Revising your story is when you make those changes. You may go through multiple rounds of review and revisions.

Writing groups can be helpful for getting feedback on your work.

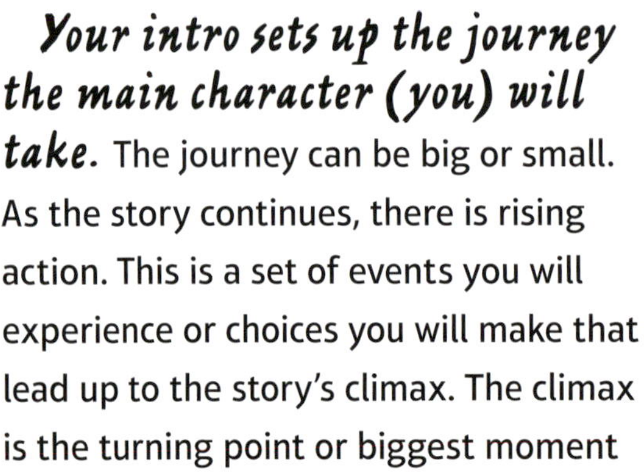

Your intro sets up the journey the main character (you) will take. The journey can be big or small. As the story continues, there is rising action. This is a set of events you will experience or choices you will make that lead up to the story's climax. The climax is the turning point or biggest moment in the story.

WRITING PROMPT: RISING ACTION

What do you think is happening in this photo? Once you decide what is happening, imagine what will happen next. That is the rising action. Write about a moment from your life. It could be similar to this photo or completely different. After you've thought about the start to your story, write about what happens next.

As you write or revise your story, think about how you are writing it. One writing technique is to show the story rather than tell it. You do this by using descriptions and sensory details that help bring your story to life. Showing the story with the five senses helps readers imagine what is happening and what you are experiencing or feeling.

WRITING PROMPT: SENSORY DETAILS AND DESCRIPTIONS

When you look at this photo, what do you see? What do you hear or smell? How would the drink taste? What would the atmosphere of the room feel like? Now think of a cozy day that you remember from your life. Use these kinds of questions to help you brainstorm ways to describe the scene of your personal narrative.

Maybe other people from your life are part of your personal narrative. If this is the case, your personal narrative may include dialogue. You can learn a lot about a person by how they respond in a conversation. Dialogue can also help show what a person is thinking or feeling.

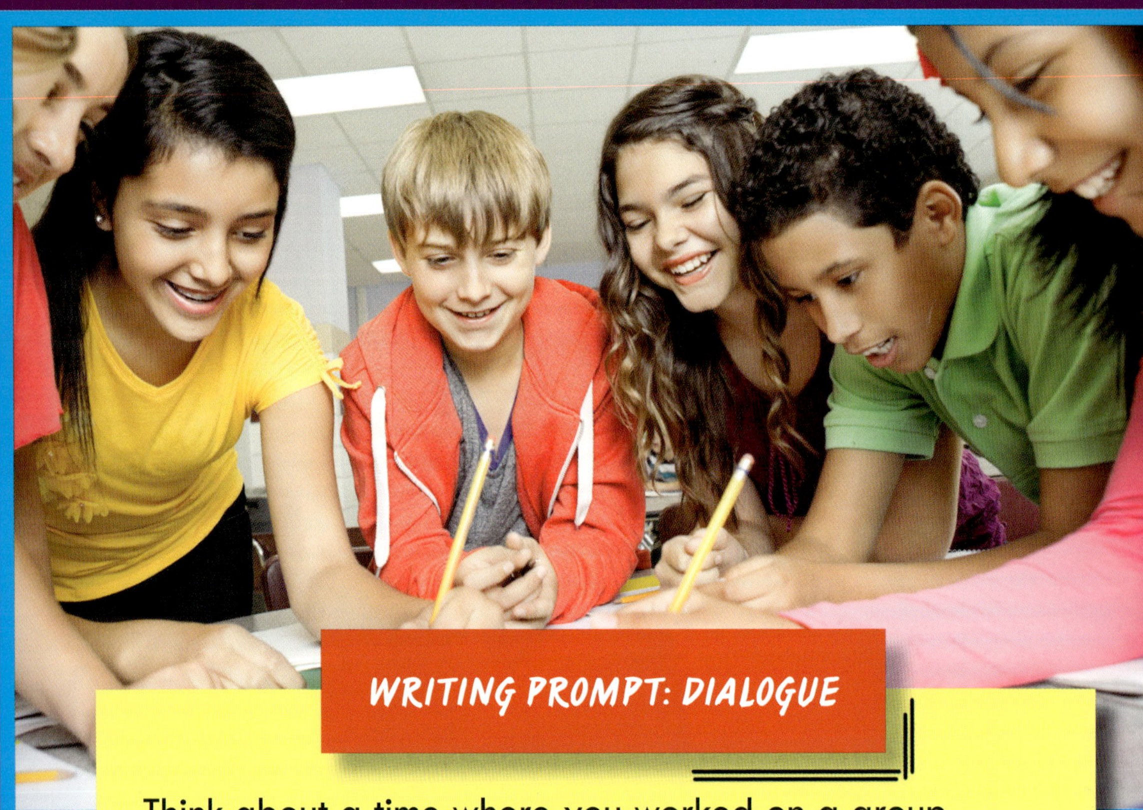

WRITING PROMPT: DIALOGUE

Think about a time where you worked on a group project at school. How did you and your group members work together? What did you say to one another as you worked? Why was your conversation important? How did you and your group members react to what other people in your group said?

Some narratives don't have dialogue. Even if your personal narrative doesn't include people talking to one another, you can still include emotions. Emotions show how you or another person from your life feels in a certain situation. Describing their or your emotions can help readers better understand or connect to the story.

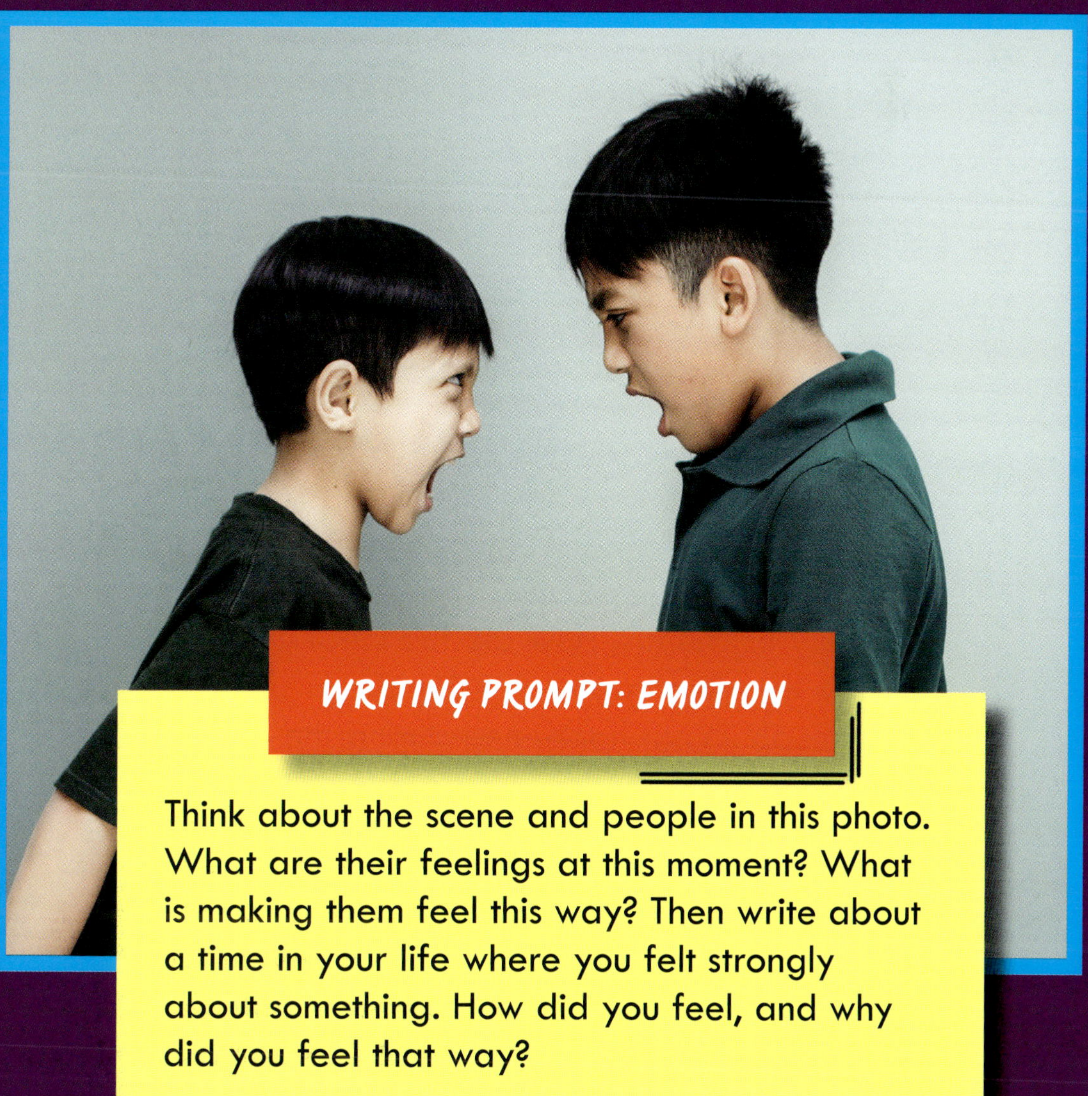

WRITING PROMPT: EMOTION

Think about the scene and people in this photo. What are their feelings at this moment? What is making them feel this way? Then write about a time in your life where you felt strongly about something. How did you feel, and why did you feel that way?

Every story includes transitions between events. One event starts the story and more events happen until the end. The number of events each story has will vary based on its length and what it's about. Some transition words and phrases, such as *next*, *then*, and *finally*, help the reader move from one event to the next. They also help show the reader how much time may be passing in the story.

WRITING PROMPT: TRANSITIONS

Write about a meal you have shared with your family or friends. How did the meal start, and who was involved? Was it a holiday meal? What happened during the meal, and how did it end? Use transition words and phrases to explain the meal's order of events in your personal narrative.

CHAPTER 3
HOW IT ENDS

Looking at photos can help stir up memories for a personal narrative.

Now it is time to make the final edits to your personal narrative. As you revise, you are likely making your story stronger. When you are done revising, read your story aloud to yourself. Does everything make sense?

Then take another look at the end of your story, which includes the falling action and resolution. Has the story come full circle? Has the character completed their journey? With an engaging conclusion, your narrative is finished.

The last step of the writing process is publishing. That means your story is ready to share with the world. Maybe you will read your story aloud to your class. You could gift your story to a friend or family member. It is also okay if you keep your story to yourself if you want.

Personal narratives can be about any element of your life, from sports to animals and more.

Remember, the climax is the biggest moment of your personal narrative. You can also think of it as the height of tension or excitement. Everything that happens after the climax is falling action. In this part of your story, you may describe actions you took based on what you've learned. You may also explain a change in yourself because of the experiences and choices you made throughout your personal narrative.

WRITING PROMPT: CLIMAX AND FALLING ACTION

If this image showed the climax of a story, how would you describe it? What would come after this moment? Now write about an exciting moment from your life. Why was it important, and what happened next?

108

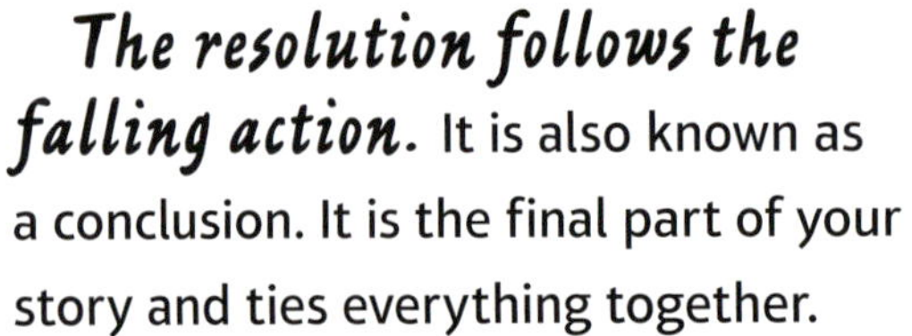

The resolution follows the falling action. It is also known as a conclusion. It is the final part of your story and ties everything together.

WRITING PROMPT: RESOLUTION

Think about a speech or presentation you have given and imagine that finishing your speech is the resolution of your personal narrative. How did you feel when you were done presenting? What did you accomplish or learn from the experience?

Maybe a set of these photos and prompts has inspired you to think more about your own life and write stories about it. You could also look through your own family photos and write a story based on one of them. Now that you know more about the writing process and have practiced writing, you can write more of your own personal narratives!

GLOSSARY

description: using words to tell readers what something is or was like in a story

dialogue: a conversation between different people in a written piece

draft: a written version of a story, or to create a written piece

editing: the process of correcting or improving a story

evaluate: to carefully review, study, or judge something, such as a story

narrator: a person or character who tells a story

outline: a written plan for a story, or to create a written plan

point of view: the perspective or view of the narrator in relation to the story

revise: to change or rewrite a story to improve it

sensory: relating to one or more of the five senses (sight, hearing, smell, taste, and touch)

technique: a method or way of doing something

transition: to move from one scene or event to the next

LEARN MORE

Britannica Kids: Storytelling
https://kids.britannica.com/kids/article/storytelling/353818

Eason, Sarah, and Louise Spilsbury. *How Do I Write Well?* Cheriton Children's Books, 2022.

Everway: 40+ Writing Prompts for Elementary Students
https://www.texthelp.com/resources/journal-prompts-for-kids/

Kiddle: List of Narrative Techniques Facts for Kids
https://kids.kiddle.co/List_of_narrative_techniques

Kiddle: Memoir Facts for Kids
https://kids.kiddle.co/Memoir

Mrs. Wordsmith. *How to Write a Story*. DK, 2022.

Rebman, Nick. *Writing in a Journal*. Focus Readers, 2024.

Schwartz, Heather E. *Writing an Opinion Piece*. Lerner Publications, 2026.

INDEX

PHOTO ACKNOWLEDGMENTS

Image credits: PeopleImages/Getty Images, p. 4; SolStock/Getty Images, p. 6; wingmar/Getty Images, p. 7; Jordan Siemens/Getty Images, p. 9; FG Trade Latin/Getty Images, p. 11; Nikada/Getty Images, p. 13; svetikd/Getty Images, p. 14; izusek/Getty Images, pp. 15, 19; Image Source/Getty Images, p. 17; SDI Productions/Getty Images, p. 20; Gatot Adriansyah/Getty Images, p. 21; Patrick Chu/Getty Images, p. 23; Jose Luis Pelaez Inc/Getty Images, p. 24; Artur Debat/Getty Images, p. 25; Caia Image/Getty Images, p. 27; Gary John Norman/Getty Images, p. 29. Design elements: Olex Runda/Shutterstock; Claudio Divizia/Shutterstock.

Cover: Marilyn Nieves/Getty Images.